Cognizanee

130 IELTS GENERAL WRITING TESTS IN ONE PRACTICE BOOK

IELTS WRITING

This book have been designed to resemble the IELTS test as closely as it can be possible. The writing tests are not, Nevertheless, real IELTS writing tests; they are designed to practice exam technique to help students face the IELTS test with confidence and to perform to the best their ability's.

General Training Task 1:

General Training Task 1

GENERAL TRAINING TASK 1 :#1

You should spend about 20 minutes on this task.

You will move to a new city for work. You know some people who live there.

In your letter,

Ask them for help finding accommodation
Tell them where you would like to live
Tell them the type of place you are looking for
Write at least 150 words.

You do NOT need to write any addresses.

Begin your letter as follows:

Dear Sir

GENERAL TRAINING TASK 1 :#2

You should spend about 20 minutes on this task.

Your car is hired from a company and while you are driving on holiday, you have a small accident. You will have to write a report to the company to explain it.
In your letter:

when and where you hired it
describe how the accident happened
what kind of action did you take after the accident
You should write at least 150 words.

You do NOT need to write your own address. Begin your letter as follows:

Dear Sir

GENERAL TRAINING TASK 1 :#3

You should spend about 20 minutes on this task.

You cannot go to a company where you got an offer. Write a letter to the HR supervisor to

explain the reason why you decline the offer
express you gratitude
explain you like your current job very much
You should write at least 150 words.

You do NOT need to write your own address. Begin your letter as follows:

Dear Sir,

GENERAL TRAINING TASK 1 :#4

You should spend about 20 minutes on this task.

You had a good meal in a local restaurant with your family. Write a letter to the newspaper to tell them about it, describe the meal you had, and why you think the restaurant is worth visiting.

You should write at least 150 words.

You do NOT need to write your own address. Begin your letter as follows:

Dear Sir,

GENERAL TRAINING TASK 1 :#5

You should spend about 20 minutes on this task.

Write a letter to complain about a situation in which some adolescents let their dogs run wildly causing dangerous.

You should write at least 150 words.

You do NOT need to write your own address. Begin your letter as follows:

Dear Sir,

GENERAL TRAINING TASK 1 :#6

You should spend about 20 minutes on this task.

You ordered a new cheque book from your bank two weeks ago but you have received nothing.

Write a letter to the manager complaining about the bad service. Say when and how you ordered the cheque book. Ask how much longer you will have to wait and ask the manager what action he will take over this matter.

You should write at least 150 words.

You do NOT need to write your own address. Begin your letter as follows:

Dear Sir,

GENERAL TRAINING TASK 1 :#7

You should spend about 20 minutes on this task.

You would like to buy some electrical goods at a shop in a nearby town.

Write a letter to the shop and ask if they have the things you want or whether they will be able to order them. Ask what the prices are and how long they will be able to hold the goods for you.

You should write at least 150 words.

You do NOT need to write your own address. Begin your letter as follows:

Dear Sir,

GENERAL TRAINING TASK 1 :#8

You should spend about 20 minutes on this task.

You have been invited to attend an interview for a place studying a course in a college. Unfortunately because of a previous appointment you cannot come at the time they wish.

Write a letter to the admissions tutor and explain your position. Apologise and offer to come on another day or later the same day. Ask also how long the interview will be and whether there will be any tests during it.

You should write at least 150 words.

You do NOT need to write your own address. Begin your letter as follows:

Dear Sir,

GENERAL TRAINING TASK 1 :#9

You should spend about 20 minutes on this task.

A friend of yours is going on holiday soon and has asked you to recommend a destination.

Write a letter to your friend and recommend a good place for a holiday that you have visited before. Say where you went, where you stayed, what you can do there and what the food was like.

You should write at least 150 words.

You do NOT need to write your own address. Begin your letter as follows:

Dear Sarah,

GENERAL TRAINING TASK 1 :#10

You should spend about 20 minutes on this task.

You have just spent a weekend at a friend's house. When you returned home, you discovered you have left a coat containing some belongings in his house.

Write a letter to your friend telling him that you left the coat. Tell him what the coat looks like, where you think you left it and what was inside it. Make some suggestions about how to get it back.

You should write at least 150 words.

You do NOT need to write your own address. Begin your letter as follows:

Dear John,

GENERAL TRAINING TASK 1 :#11

You should spend about 20 minutes on this task.

You live in a room in college which you share with another student. You find it very difficult to work there because he or she always has friends visiting. They have parties in the room and sometimes borrow your things without asking you.

Write a letter to the Accommodation Officer at the college and ask for a new room next term. You would prefer a single room. Explain your reasons.

You should write at least 150 words.

You do NOT need to write your own address. Begin your letter as follows:

Dear Sir/Madam,

GENERAL TRAINING TASK 1 :#12

You should spend about 20 minutes on this task.

You have heard that a developer plans to build a shopping centre near your home.

Write a letter to the council. In your letter

say how you heard about the plan
explain how you feel about it
ask for more information about it
Write at least 150 words.

You do NOT need to write any addresses.

Begin your letter as follows:

Dear Sir or Madam,

GENERAL TRAINING TASK 1 :#13

You should spend about 20 minutes on this task.

You recently bought a camera while travelling overseas. When you got to your destination you discovered that some important items were missing from the box.

Write a letter to the local representative of the company. In your letter

give details of the camera and where you bought it
explain what has happened
say what you want him/her to do about it
Write at least 150 words
You do NOT need to write any addresses.

Begin your letter as follows:

Dear Sir or Madam,

GENERAL TRAINING TASK 1 :#14

You should spend about 20 minutes on this task.

You are currently taking a course at a college but you will need to h week off during this course.

Write a letter to the college Principal. In the letter

give details of your course
explain why you need a week off
say what you want the Principal to do.
Write at least 150 words.

You do NOT need to write any addresses.

Begin your letter as follows:

Dear Sir or Madam,

GENERAL TRAINING TASK 1 :#15

You should spend about 20 minutes on this task.

You are renting a flat from an agency. Your contract was for one year but you need to leave the flat two months early.

Write a letter to the agency. In your letter

introduce yourself
ask to leave the flat before the contract finishes
explain why you need to break the contract.
Write at least 150 words.

You do NOT need to write any addresses.

Begin your letter as follows:

Dear Sir or Madam,

GENERAL TRAINING TASK 1 :#16

You should spend about 20 minutes on this task.

You paid a refundable deposit when you rented an apartment. You left the apartment in good condition but the Landlord won't return your deposit.

Write a letter to the landlord. In your letter

explain why you are writing
ask for the return of your deposit
inform the landlord of possible legal action
Write at least 150 words.

You do NOT need to write any addresses.

Begin your letter as follows:

Dear Sir or Madam,

GENERAL TRAINING TASK 1 :#17

You should spend about 20 minutes on this task.

There is a public park near where you live. You have heard that the local council wants to sell this park.

Write a letter to a local newspaper. In your letter:

introduce yourself
describe the importance of the park
say what action you will take if the council continues with its plan
Write at least 150 words.

You do NOT need to write any addresses.

Begin your letter as follows:

Dear Sir or Madam,

GENERAL TRAINING TASK 1 :#19

You should spend about 20 minutes on this task.

You arranged to visit a friend in Canada but an important event at home now means that you must change the dates of the visit.

Write a letter to your friend. In your letter

explain the important event
apologise for the situation
suggest a new arrangement
Write at least 150 words.

You do NOT need to write any addresses.

Begin your letter as follows:

Dear Sir or Madam,

GENERAL TRAINING TASK 1 :#20

You should spend about 20 minutes on this task.

You are a student at a language school in New Zealand studying Business English. Part of the course is a summer work placement programme. Unfortunately, you have just learnt from the school that this programme has now been cancelled.

Write a letter to the School Principal. In your letter:

state your reason for writing
describe the problem and your concerns
explain what you would like the Principal to do.
Write at least 150 words.

You do NOT need to write any addresses.
Begin your letter as follows:

Dear Sir or Madam,

GENERAL TRAINING TASK 1 :#21

You should spend about 20 minutes on this task.

Last Wednesday you flew from London to Vancouver. When you arrived home, you discovered that you had left your hand luggage on the plane.

Write a letter to the airline. In your letter, you should explain:

where and when you lost your bag
what your bag looks like
what its contents were
Write at least 150 words.

You do NOT need to write any addresses.

Begin your letter as follows:

Dear Sir or Madam,

GENERAL TRAINING TASK 1 :#22

You should spend about 20 minutes on this task.

You have seen an advertisement for a community college that needs teachers for night classes.

Write a letter to the community college. In your letter:

say which advertisement you are answering
describe which course(s) you want to teach, and what it/they would be about
explain why you would be a suitable teacher
Write at least 150 words.

You do NOT need to write any addresses

Begin your letter as follows:

Dear Sir or Madam,

GENERAL TRAINING TASK 1 :#23

You should spend about 20 minutes on this task.

A restaurant has placed an advertisement for waiters and waitresses in your local newspaper.

Write a letter to the restaurant, applying for the job. In your letter:

explain what you are currently doing
describe your suitability for this area of work
say when you can attend an interview
Write at least 150 words.

You do NOT need to write any addresses.

Begin your letter as follows:

Dear Sir or Madam,

GENERAL TRAINING TASK 1 :#24

You should spend about 20 minutes on this task.

You are studying for a qualification, and you would like some time off work to complete it.

Write a letter to your manager. In your letter:

Ask for some time off to complete a qualification.
Suggest what you will do later at work if you have time off.
Say how the qualification helps your job or company.
Write at least 150 words.

You do NOT need to write any addresses.

Begin your letter as follows:

Dear Sir or Madam,

GENERAL TRAINING TASK 1 :#25

You should spend about 20 minutes on this task.

You play a team sport with some friends. Last week a member of the team had an accident and wasn't able to play with you at the weekend. You decide to write to him in hospital, telling him about the match.

Write a letter to your friend. In your letter,

tell him which team won
describe the conditions on the day
say how you felt about the match
Write at least 150 words.

You do NOT need to write any addresses.

Begin your letter as follows:

Dear Sir or Madam,

GENERAL TRAINING TASK 1 :#26

You should spend about 20 minutes on this task.

You are going to another country to study. You would like to do a part-time job while you are studying, so you want to ask a friend who lives there for some help.

Write a letter to your friend. In your letter,

give details of your study plans
explain why you want to get a part-time job
suggest how your friend could help you find a job
Write at least 150 words.

You do NOT need to write any addresses.

Begin your letter as follows:

Dear Sir or Madam,

GENERAL TRAINING TASK 1 :#27

You should spend about 20 minutes on this task.

You are studying a short course in another country. Your accommodation was arranged by the course provider. There is a major problem with the accommodation.

Write a letter to the course provider. In your letter,

say what the problem is
describe the accommodation you thought you were getting
ask the provider to solve the problem
Write at least 150 words.

You do NOT need to write any addresses.
Begin your letter as follows:

Dear Sir or Madam,

GENERAL TRAINING TASK 1 :#28

You should spend about 20 minutes on this task.

You have seen an advertisement in an English newspaper for a job working in the City Museum shop during the holidays. You decide to apply for the job.

Write a letter to the director of the Museum. In your letter,

introduce yourself
explain what experience and special skills you have
explain why you are interested in the job
Write at least 150 words.

You do NOT need to write any addresses.

Begin your letter as follows:

Dear Sir or Madam,

GENERAL TRAINING TASK 1 :#29

You should spend about 20 minutes on this task.

You are looking for a part-time job at a football club.

Write a letter to the manager of the football club. In your letter,

introduce yourself
explain what experience and special skills you have
tell him/her when you think you could start
Write at least 150 words.

You do NOT need to write any addresses.

Begin your letter as follows:

Dear Sir or Madam,

GENERAL TRAINING TASK 1 :#30

You should spend about 20 minutes on this task.

You saw an advertisement for a tennis course in England but you have one or two problems and can't stay the whole course.

Write a letter to the course director. In your letter,

explain your interest in the course
describe your problems
find out if a refund is possible
Write at least 150 words.

You do NOT need to write any addresses.

Begin your letter as follows:

Dear Sir or Madam,

GENERAL TRAINING TASK 1 :#31

You should spend about 20 minutes on this task.

You are due to move into a rented apartment next month but be able to because you have some problems.

Write a letter to the course provider. In your letter,

explain your situation
describe your problems
tell him/her when you think you can move in
Write at least 150 words.

You do NOT need to write any addresses.

Begin your letter as follows:

Dear Sir or Madam,

GENERAL TRAINING TASK 1 :#32

You should spend about 20 minutes on this task.

You are a student at an English language school in Brighton and are living in private accommodation with other flat mates. You have not had hot water or heating for some time. The landlord's workmen have tried to fix the problem but without success.

Write a letter to the landlord. In your letter,

state your reason for writing
describe the problems and explain how you feel
propose a solution and risk the landlord to take action
Write at least 150 words.

You do NOT need to write any addresses.

Begin your letter as follows:

Dear Sir or Madam,

GENERAL TRAINING TASK 1 :#33

You should spend about 20 minutes on this task.

You are going on a short course to a training college abroad. It is a college that you have not been to before.

Write a letter to the accommodation officer. In your letter,

give details of your course and your arrival/departure date
explain your accommodation needs
ask for information about getting to and from the college
Write at least 150 words.

You do NOT need to write any addresses.

Begin your letter as follows:

Dear ....

GENERAL TRAINING TASK 1 :#34

You should spend about 20 minutes on this task.

You are looking for a part-time job.

Write a letter to an employment agency. In your letter,

introduce yourself
explain what sort of job you would like
and say what experience and skills you have
Write at least 150 words.

You do NOT need to write any addresses.

Begin your letter as follows:

Dear .... ,

GENERAL TRAINING TASK 1 :#35

You should spend about 20 minutes on this task.

You are going on a short training course at a collage in Greenmount, Northern Ireland. You need somewhere to live while you are there.

Write a letter to the accommodation officer at the college. In your letter,

explain your situation
describe the accommodation you require
say when you will need it
Write at least 150 words.

You do NOT need to write any addresses.

Begin your letter as follows:

Dear Ms Rose

GENERAL TRAINING TASK 1 :#36

You should spend about 20 minutes on this task.

An English-speaking friend wants to spend a two-week holiday in your region and has written asking for information and advice.

Write a letter to your friend. In your letter,

offer to find somewhere to stay
give advice about what to do
give information about what clothes to bring
Write at least 150 words.

You do NOT need to write any addresses.

Begin your letter as follows:

Dear ....

GENERAL TRAINING TASK 1 :#37

You should spend about 20 minutes on this task.

You eat at your college cafeteria every lunchtime. However, you think it needs some improvements.

Write a letter to the college magazine. In your letter,

explain what you like about the cafeteria
say what is wrong with it
suggest how it could be improved
Write at least 150 words.

You do NOT need to write any addresses.

Begin your letter as follows:

Dear ....

GENERAL TRAINING TASK 1 :#38

You should spend about 20 minutes on this task.

You have a full time job and are also doing a part time evening course. You now find that you can not continue the course.

Write a letter to your tutor. In your letter,

describe the situation
explain why you cannot continue at this time
say what action you would like to take
Write at least 150 words.

You do NOT need to write any addresses.

Begin your letter as follows:

Dear ....

GENERAL TRAINING TASK 1 :#39

You should spend about 20 minutes on this task.

Your neighbours have recently written to you to complain about the noise from your house/flat.

Write a letter to your neighbours. In your letter,

explain the reasons for the noise
apologise
describe what action you will take
Write at least 150 words.

You do NOT need to write any addresses.

Begin your letter as follows:

Dear ....

GENERAL TRAINING TASK 1 :#40

You have recently heard that a friend of yours has had some problems as a result of some unusual weather. Write a letter to your friend.
In your letter

express concern (i.e. say you are sorry to hear what has happened)
tell them about a similar experience that you once had
give some advice or offer help
You should write at least 80 words.
Allow yourself 15 minutes for this task.

Begin your letter as follows:

Dear ....

GENERAL TRAINING TASK 1 :#41

You recently visited a place that had a strong impact on you.
Write a letter to a friend about the place. In your letter explain where the place was and how you got there describe what you
 saw offer to take your friend there

You do NOT need to write any addresses.

Begin your letter as follows:

Dear ....

GENERAL TRAINING TASK 1 :#42

You recently took a part-time job working for a local company. After a few weeks, you realised there were some problems with the job.
Write a letter to the manager of the company. In your letter explain why you took the job describe the problems that you experienced suggest what could be done about them
You do NOT need to write any addresses.

Begin your letter as follows:

Dear ....

GENERAL TRAINING TASK 1 :#43

A friend has asked you to babysit on Saturday and wants to know how much you charge per hour for this. Unfortunately, you already have a commitment this weekend and cannot help. However, you free the following weekend.
Write a letter to your friend exlaining that you are not able to help this time, but could help later. Explain also what your fee for the service is.

You should write at least 150 words.
You should spend about 20 minutes on this task.
You do NOT need to write any addresses.

Begin your letter as follows:

Dear ....

GENERAL TRAINING TASK 1 : #44

You have just rented an unfurnished flat and a friend has told you that the Opportunity Shop in the shoping centre has cheap second-hand furniture. Write to the shop owner describing what you need and asking whether they have these items and what they cost.

You should write at least 150 words.
You should spend about 20 minutes on this task.
You do not need to write your own address
Begin your letter as follows:

Dear ....

GENERAL TRAINING TASK 1 : #45

You are an international student and have borrowed a book from the local public library.
You left the book on a bus and when you contacted the bus company, they could not find it.

Write a letter to the librarian explaining the situation and asking what you should do.

You should write at least 150 words.
You should spend about 20 minutes on this task.
Begin your letter as follows:
Dear ....

GENERAL TRAINING TASK 1 : #46

You celebrated your birthday with some friends last week in a restaurant. It was a great success and you and your friends enjoyed the evening very much.
Write a letter to the restaurant to thank them. Mention the food, service and the atmosphere. Also suggest any improvements to make things better.

You should write at least 150 words.
You should spend about 20 minutes on this task.
You do NOT need to write your own address
Begin your letter as follows:
Dear ....

GENERAL TRAINING TASK 1 :#47

You are going to study in a college in the UK next year. You would like to stay in a college Hall of Residence.

Write a letter to the college giving your accommodation requirements. You should outline what your room and food needs are and also ask what alternatives are available if they cannot provide what you want.

You should write at least 150 words.
You should spend about 20 minutes on this task.
You do NOT need to write your own address.
Begin your letter as follows:

Dear ....

GENERAL TRAINING TASK 1 :#48

Last week you were on a flight to London. Unfortunately, when you left the plane, you left a bag. You did not remember about the bag until you got to your hotel.

Write a letter to the airline. Explain what has happened, describe the bag and its contents and say what you would like them to do about it.

You should write at least 150 words.
You should spend about 20 minutes on this task.
You do NOT need to write your own address.
Begin your letter as follows:

Dear ....

GENERAL TRAINING TASK 1 :#49

You have just returned home after living with a family in an English-speaking country for six months.
You now realise that you left a small bag of personal possessions in your room.
Write to the family describing the things you left behind. Ask them to send some ar all of them to you. Offer to cover the costs.

You should write at least 150 words.
You should spend about 20 minutes on this task.
You do NOT need to write your own address.
Begin your letter as follows:
Dear ....

GENERAL TRAINING TASK 1 :#50

You are unhappy about a plan to make your local airport bigger and increase the number of flights. You live near the airport.
Write a letter to your local newspaper. In your letter:

- explain where you live
- describe the problem
- give reasons why you do not want this development.

You should write at least 150 words.
You should spend about 20 minutes on this task.
You do NOT need to write your own address.
Begin your letter as follows:

Dear ....

General Training Task 2:

General Training Task 2:

GENERAL TRAINING TASK 2: #7

You should spend about 40 minutes on this task.

Write about the following topic:

Social media is becoming increasingly popular amongst all age groups. However, sharing personal information on social media websites does have risks.

Do you think that the advantages of social media outweigh the disadvantages?

Give reasons for your answer and include any relevant examples from your own knowledge or experience.

Write at least 250 words.

GENERAL TRAINING TASK 2: #8

You should spend about 40 minutes on this task.

Write about the following topic:

Some people think that developed countries have a higher responsibility to combat climate change than developing countries. Others believe that all countries should have the same responsibilities towards protecting the environment.

Discuss both these views and give your own opinion.

Write at least 250 words.

Give reasons for your answer and include any relevant examples from your own knowledge or experience.

GENERAL TRAINING TASK 2: #9

You should spend about 40 minutes on this task.

Write about the following topic:

A government's role is only to provide defence capability and urban infrastructure (roads, water supplies, etc.). All other services (education, health, social security) should be provided by private groups or individuals in the community.

Discuss both these views and give your own opinion.

Write at least 250 words.

Give reasons for your answer and include any relevant examples from your own knowledge or experience

---

GENERAL TRAINING TASK 2: #10

You should spend about 40 minutes on this task.

Write about the following topic:

In the past, shopping was a routine domestic task. Many people nowadays regard it as a hobby.

To what extent do you think this is a positive trend?

Give reasons for your answer and include any relevant examples from your own knowledge or experience.

Write at least 250 words.

GENERAL TRAINING TASK 2: #11

You should spend about 40 minutes on this task.

Write about the following topic:

Genetic engineering is a dangerous trend. It should be limited.
To what extent do you agree?

Give reasons for your answer and include any relevant examples from your own knowledge or experience.

Write at least 250 words.

GENERAL TRAINING TASK 2: #12

You should spend about 40 minutes on this task.

Write about the following topic:

Should the international community do more to tackle the threat of global warming?

Give reasons for your answer and include any relevant examples from your own knowledge or experience.

Write at least 250 words.

GENERAL TRAINING TASK 2: #13

You should spend about 40 minutes on this task.

Write about the following topic:

Many people believe that increasing levels of violence on television and in films is having a direct result on levels of violence in society. Others claim that violence in society is the result of more fundamental social problems such as unemployment.
How much do you think society is affected by violence in the media?

Give reasons for your answer and include any relevant examples from your own knowledge or experience.

Write at least 250 words.

GENERAL TRAINING TASK 2: #14

You should spend about 40 minutes on this task.

Write about the following topic:

Compare the advantages and disadvantages of three of the following ways of learning a foreign language.

State which you consider to be the most effective.

studying on your own
taking lessons with a private tutor
taking lessons as part of a class
taking lessons online
going to live in a country where the language is spoken
Give reasons for your answer and include any relevant examples from your own knowledge or experience.

Write at least 250 words.

GENERAL TRAINING TASK 2: #15

You should spend about 40 minutes on this task.

Write about the following topic:

Governments around the world spend too much money on treating illnesses and diseases and not enough on health education and prevention.

Do you agree or disagree with this statement?

Give reasons for your answer and include any relevant examples from your own knowledge or experience.

Write at least 250 words.

GENERAL TRAINING TASK 2: #16

You should spend about 40 minutes on this task.

Write about the following topic:

Today's teenagers have more stressful lives than previous generations.

Discuss this view and give your own opinion.

Give reasons for your answer and include any relevant examples from your own knowledge or experience.

Write at least 250 words.

GENERAL TRAINING TASK 2: #17

You should spend about 40 minutes on this task.

Write about the following topic:

In some countries it is thought advisable that children begin formal education at four years old, while in others they do not have to start school until they are seven or eight.

How far do you agree with either of these views?

Give reasons for your answer and include any relevant examples from your own knowledge or experience.

Write at least 250 words

GENERAL TRAINING TASK 2: #18

You should spend about 40 minutes on this task.

Write about the following topic:

Women are better at childcare than men therefore they should focus more on raising children and less on their working life.

To what extent do you agree or disagree with this statement?

Give reasons for your answer and include any relevant examples from your own knowledge or experience.

GENERAL TRAINING TASK 2: #19

You should spend about 40 minutes on this task.

Write about the following topic:

Increasing numbers of students are choosing to study abroad.

To what extent does this trend benefit the students themselves and the countries involved?

What are the drawbacks?

Give reasons for your answer and include any relevant examples from your own knowledge or experience.

Write at least 250 words

GENERAL TRAINING TASK 2: #20

You should spend about 40 minutes on this task.

Write about the following topic:

Many people believe that the high levels of violence in films today are causing serious social problems.

What are these problems and how could they be reduced?

Give reasons for your answer and include any relevant examples from your own knowledge or experience.

Write at least 250 words

GENERAL TRAINING TASK 2: #21

You should spend about 40 minutes on this task.

Write about the following topic:

Car ownership has increased so rapidly over the past thirty years that many cities in the world are now 'one big traffic jam'.

How true do you think this statement is? What measures can governments take to discourage people from using their cars?

Give reasons for your answer and include any relevant examples from your own knowledge or experience.

Write at least 250 words

GENERAL TRAINING TASK 2: #22

You should spend about 40 minutes on this task.

Write about the following topic:

Longer life spans and improvements in the health of older people suggest that people over the age of sixty-five can continue to live full and active lives.

In what ways can society benefit from the contribution that older people can make?

Give reasons for your answer and include any relevant examples from your own knowledge or experience.

Write at least 250 words.

GENERAL TRAINING TASK 2: #23

You should spend about 40 minutes on this task.

Write about the following topic:

In the modern world, the image (photograph or film) is becoming a more powerful way of communicating than the written word.

To what extent do you agree or disagree?

Give reasons for your answer and include any relevant examples from your own knowledge or experience.

Write at least 250 words

GENERAL TRAINING TASK 2: #24

You should spend about 40 minutes on this task.

Write about the following topic:

Supermarkets should only sell food produced from within their own country rather than imports from overseas.

What are your opinions on this?

Give reasons for your answer and include any relevant examples from your own knowledge or experience.

Write at least 250 words.

GENERAL TRAINING TASK 2: #25

You should spend about 40 minutes on this task.

Write about the following topic:

In the past, shopping was a routine domestic task. Many people nowadays regard it as a hobby.

To what extent do you think this is a positive trend?

Give reasons for your answer and include any relevant examples from your own knowledge or experience.

Write at least 250 words

GENERAL TRAINING TASK 2: #26

You should spend about 40 minutes on this task.

Write about the following topic:

Advances in science and technology and other areas of society in the last 100 years have transformed the way we live as well as postponing the day we die. There is no better lime to be alive than now.

To what extent do you agree or disagree with this opinion?

Give reasons for your answer and include any relevant examples from your own knowledge or experience.

Write at least 250 words.

GENERAL TRAINING TASK 2: #27

You should spend about 40 minutes on this task.

Write about the following topic:

The most important consideration when choosing any career or job is having a high income.

To what extent do you agree or disagree?

Give reasons for your answer and include any relevant examples from your own knowledge or experience.

Write at least 250 words

GENERAL TRAINING TASK 2: #28

You should spend about 40 minutes on this task.

Write about the following topic:

Most people do not care enough about environmental issues.

To what extent do you agree or disagree?

Give reasons for your answer and include any relevant examples from your own knowledge or experience.

Write at least 250 words

GENERAL TRAINING TASK 2: #29

You should spend about 40 minutes on this task.

Write about the following topic:

Very few schoolchildren learn about the value of money and how to look after it, yet this is a critical life skill that should be taught as part of the school curriculum.

Do you agree or disagree?

Give reasons for your answer and include any relevant examples from your own knowledge or experience.

Write at least 250 words.

GENERAL TRAINING TASK 2: #30

You should spend about 40 minutes on this task.

Write about the following topic:

Many students choose to take a gap year before starting university, to travel or gain work experience.

Do you think this is a good idea or a waste of time?

Give reasons for your answer and include any relevant examples from your own knowledge or experience.

Write at least 250 words.

GENERAL TRAINING TASK 2: #31

You should spend about 40 minutes on this task.

Present a written argument or case to an educated reader with no specialist knowledge of the following topic.

Many childhood diseases can now be prevented through the use of vaccines.

Should parents be made by law to immunise their children against common diseases or should individuals have the right to choose not to immunise their children?

You should use your own ideas, knowledge and experience and support your arguments with examples and relevant evidence.

You should write at least 250 words

GENERAL TRAINING TASK 2: #32

You should spend about 40 minutes on this task.

Present a written argument or case to an educated reader with no specialist knowledge of the following topic.

In some countries an increasing number of people are suffering from health problems as a result of eating too much fast food. It is therefore necessary for governments to impose a higher tax on this kind of food.

To what extent do you agree or disagree with this opinion?

You should use your own ideas, knowledge and experience and support your arguments with examples and relevant evidence.

You should write at least 250 words.

GENERAL TRAINING TASK 2: #33

You should spend about 40 minutes on this task.

Present a written argument or case to an educated reader with no specialist knowledge of the following topic.

Film stars and music celebrities may earn a great deal of money and live in luxurious surroundings, but many of them lead unhappy lives. Do you agree?

To what extent is this the price they pay for being famous?

You should use your own ideas, knowledge and experience and support your arguments with examples and relevant evidence.

You should write at least 250 words.

GENERAL TRAINING TASK 2: #34

You should spend about 40 minutes on this task.

In today's job market it is far more important to have practical skills than theoretical knowledge. In the future, job applicants may not need any formal qualifications.

To what extent do you agree or disagree?

Write at least 250 words.

GENERAL TRAINING TASK 2: #35

You should spend about 40 minutes on this task.

Motorways help people travel quickly and cover long distances but they also cause problems. What are the problems of motorways and what solutions are there?

Give reasons for your answer and include any relevant examples from your own knowledge or experience.

Write at least 250 words.

GENERAL TRAINING TASK 2: #36

You should spend about 40 minutes on this task.

It is generally believed that the Internet is an excellent means of communication but some people suggest that it may not be the best place to find information.

Discuss both these views and give your own opinion.

Write at least 250 words.

GENERAL TRAINING TASK 2: #37

You should spend about 40 minutes on this task.

Celebrities make a very good living out of media attention and have chosen to live in the public spotlight. They have no right to complain when they feel the media are intruding on their privacy.

To what extent do you agree or disagree with this opinion?

Write at least 250 words.

GENERAL TRAINING TASK 2: #38

You should spend about 40 minutes on this task.

Write about the following topic:

Some parents buy their children a large number of toys to play with.

What are the advantages and disadvantages for the child of having a large number of toys?

Give reasons for your answer and include any relevant examples from your own knowledge or experience.

Write at least 250 words.

GENERAL TRAINING TASK 2: #39

You should spend about 40 minutes on this task.

Write about the following topic:

In general, people do not have such a close relationship with their neighbours as they did in the past.

Why is this so, and what can be done to improve contact between neighbours?

Give reasons for your answer and include any relevant examples from your own knowledge or experience.

Write at least 250 words.

GENERAL TRAINING TASK 2: #40

You should spend about 40 minutes on this task.

Write about the following topic:

Some people think that human history has been a journey from ignorance to knowledge. Others argue that this underestimates the achievements of ancient cultures, and overvalues our achievements.

Discuss both these views and give your own opinion.

Write at least 250 words.

GENERAL TRAINING TASK 2: #41

You should spend about 40 minutes on this task.

Write about the following topic:

Some people think that there are things individuals can do to help prevent global climate change. Others believe that action by individuals is useless and irrelevant and that it is only governments and large businesses which can make a difference.

Discuss both these views and give your own opinion.

Write at least 250 words.

GENERAL TRAINING TASK 2: #42

You should spend about 40 minutes on this task.

Write about the following topic:

Many people believe that media coverage of celebrities is having a negative effect on children.
To what extent do you agree or disagree with this statement?

Give reasons for your answer and include any relevant examples from your own knowledge or experience.
Write at least 250 words

GENERAL TRAINING TASK 2: #43

You should spend about 40 minutes on this task.

Write about the following topic:

Many high-level positions in companies are filled by men even though the workforce in many developed countries is more than 50 per cent female. Companies should be required to allocate a certain percentage of these positions to women.

To what extent do you agree?

Write at least 250 words.

GENERAL TRAINING TASK 2: #44

You should spend about 40 minutes on this task.

Write about the following topic:

Some people think that professional athletes make good role models for young people, while others believe they don't.

Discuss both these points of views and give your own opinion.

Write at least 250 words.

GENERAL TRAINING TASK 2: #45

You should spend about 40 minutes on this task.

Write about the following topic:

Is freedom of speech necessary in a free society?

Give reasons for your answer.

Write at least 250 words.

GENERAL TRAINING TASK 2: #46

You should spend about 40 minutes on this task.

Write about the following topic:

Some people think women should be allowed to join the army, the navy and the air force just like men.

To what extent do you agree or disagree?

Write at least 250 words.

GENERAL TRAINING TASK 2: #47

You should spend about 40 minutes on this task.

Write about the following topic:

Machine translation (MT) is slower and less accurate than human translation and there is no immediate or predictable likelihood of machines taking over this role from humans.
Do you agree or disagree?

Write at least 250 words.

GENERAL TRAINING TASK 2: #48

You should spend about 40 minutes on this task.

Write about the following topic:

Many newspapers and magazines feature stories about the private lives of famous people. We know what they eat, where they buy their clothes and who they love. We also often see pictures of them in private situations.

Is it appropriate for a magazine or newspaper to give this kind of private information about people?

Give reasons for your answer.

Write at least 250 words.

GENERAL TRAINING TASK 2: #49

You should spend about 40 minutes on this task.

Write about the following topic:

Some people feel that certain workers like nurses, doctors and teachers are undervalued and should be paid more, especially when other people like film actors or company bosses are paid huge sums of money that are out of proportion to the importance of the work that they do.

How far do you agree?
What criteria should be used to decide how much people are paid?
You should use your own ideas, knowledge and experience and support your arguments with examples and relevant evidence.

Write at least 250 words.

GENERAL TRAINING TASK 2: #50

You should spend about 40 minutes on this task.

Write about the following topic:

Some people consider computers to be more of a hindrance than a help. Others believe that they have greatly increased human potential.

How could computers be considered a hindrance?

Give reasons for your answer and include any relevant examples from your own experience.

Write at least 250 words.

GENERAL TRAINING TASK 2: #51

You should spend about 40 minutes on this task.

Write about the following topic:

Modern lifestyles mean that many parents have little time for their children. Many children suffer because they do not get as much attention from their parents as children did in the past.

Do you agree or disagree?

Give reasons for your answer and include any relevant examples from your own experience.

Write at least 250 words.

GENERAL TRAINING TASK 2: #52

You should spend about 40 minutes on this task.

Write about the following topic:

In most countries multinational companies and their products are becoming more and more important. This trend is seriously damaging our quality of life.

Do you agree or disagree?

Give reasons for your answer and include any relevant examples from your own experience.

Write at least 250 words.

GENERAL TRAINING TASK 2: #53

You should spend about 40 minutes on this task.

Write about the following topic:

More and more qualified people are moving from poor to rich countries to fill vacancies in specialist areas like engineering, computing and medicine.

Some people believe that by encouraging the movement of such people, rich countries are stealing from poor countries. Others feel that this is only part of the natural movement of workers around the world.

Do you agree or disagree?

Give reasons for your answer and include any relevant examples from your own experience.

Write at least 250 words.

GENERAL TRAINING TASK 2: #54

You should spend about 40 minutes on this task.

Write about the following topic:

Nowadays many students have the opportunity to study for part or all of their courses in foreign countries.

While studying abroad brings many benefits to individual students, it also has a number of disadvantages.

Do you agree or disagree?

Give reasons for your answer and include any relevant examples from your own experience.

Write at least 250 words.

GENERAL TRAINING TASK 2: #56

You should spend about 40 minutes on this task.

Write about the following topic:

As mass communication and transport continue to grow, societies are becoming more and more alike leading to a phenomenon known as globalization. Some people fear that globalization will inevitably lead to the total loss of cultural identity.

To what extent do you agree or disagree with this statement?

Give reasons for your answer and include any relevant examples from your own knowledge or experience.

Write at least 250 words.

GENERAL TRAINING TASK 2: #57

You should spend about 40 minutes on this task.

Write about the following topic:

In some countries young people have little leisure time and are under a lot of pressure to work hard in their studies.

What do you think are the causes of this? What solutions can you suggest?

Give reasons for your answer and include any relevant examples from your own knowledge or experience.

Write at least 250 words.

GENERAL TRAINING TASK 2: #58

You should spend about 40 minutes on this task.

Write about the following topic:

Computers and modems have made it possible for office workers to do much of their work from home instead of working in offices every day. Working from home should be encouraged as it is good for workers and employers.

Do you agree or disagree?

Give reasons for your answer and include any relevant examples from your own experience.

Write at least 250 words.

GENERAL TRAINING TASK 2: #59

You should spend about 40 minutes on this task.

Write about the following topic:

It is becoming more and more difficult to escape the influence of the media on our lives.

Discuss the advantages and disadvantages of living in a media rich society.

Give reasons for your answer and include any relevant examples from your own knowledge or experience.

Write at least 250 words.

GENERAL TRAINING TASK 2: #60

You should spend about 40 minutes on this task.

Write about the following topic:

Many people say that the only way to guarantee getting a good job is to complete a course of university education. Others claim that it is better to start work after school and gain experience in the world of work.

How far do you agree or disagree with the above views?

Give reasons for your answer and include any relevant examples from your own knowledge or experience.

Write at least 250 words.

GENERAL TRAINING TASK 2: #61

You should spend about 40 minutes on this task.

Do you agree or disagree with the following statement?
Television has destroyed communication among friends and family.
Use specific reasons and examples to support your opinion.

You should write at least 250 words.

Give reasons for your answer and include any relevant examples from your own knowledge or experience

---

GENERAL TRAINING TASK 2: #62

You should spend about 40 minutes on this task.

We all work or will work in our jobs with many different kinds of people. In your opinion, what are some important characteristics of a co-worker (someone you work closely with)?
Use reasons and specific examples to explain why these characteristics are important.

You should write at least 250 words.

GENERAL TRAINING TASK 2: #63

You should spend about 40 minutes on this task.

Do you agree or disagree with the following statement?
Classmates are a more important influence than parents on a child's success in school.
Use specific reasons and examples to support your answer.

You should write at least 250 words.

GENERAL TRAINING TASK 2: #64

You should spend about 40 minutes on this task.

It is better for children to grow up in the countryside than in a big city.
Do you agree or disagree?
Use specific reasons and examples to develop your essay.

You should write at least 250 words.

GENERAL TRAINING TASK 2: #65

You should spend about 40 minutes on this task.

A person you know is planning to move to your town or city. What do you think this person would like and dislike about living in your town or city? Why? Use specific reasons and details to develop your essay.

You should write at least 250 words.

GENERAL TRAINING TASK 2: #66

You should spend about 40 minutes on this task.

Some people think that children should begin their formal education at a very early age and should spend most of their time on school studies. Others believe that young children should spend most of their time playing.
Compare these two views. Which view do you agree with? Why?

You should write at least 250 words.

GENERAL TRAINING TASK 2: #67

You should spend about 40 minutes on this task.

Do you agree or disagree with the following statement?
Watching television is bad for children.
Use specific reasons and examples to support your opinion.

You should write at least 250 words.

GENERAL TRAINING TASK 2: #68

You should spend about 40 minutes on this task.

Do you agree or disagree with the following statement?
Children should begin learning a foreign language as soon as they start school.
Use specific reasons and examples to support your opinion.

You should write at least 250 words.

GENERAL TRAINING TASK 2: #69

You should spend about 40 minutes on this task.

It is better for children to grow up in the countryside than in a big city.
Do you agree or disagree?
Use specific reasons and examples to develop your essay.

You should write at least 250 words.

GENERAL TRAINING TASK 2: #70

You should spend about 40 minutes on this task.

Do you agree or disagree with the following statement?
Parents or other adult relatives should make important decisions for their (15 to 18 year-old) teenage children.
Use specific reasons and examples to support your opinion.

You should write at least 250 words.

GENERAL TRAINING TASK 2: #71

You should spend about 40 minutes on this task.

Do you agree or disagree with the following statement?
Children should be required to help with household tasks as soon as they are able to do so.
Use specific reasons and examples to support your answer.

You should write at least 250 words.

GENERAL TRAINING TASK 2: #72

You should spend about 40 minutes on this task.

What are some important qualities of a good supervisor (boss)?
Use specific details and examples to explain why these qualities are important.

You should write at least 250 words.

GENERAL TRAINING TASK 2: #73

You should spend about 40 minutes on this task.

Some people enjoy change, and they look forward to new experiences. Others like their lives to stay the same, and they do not change their usual habits.
Compare these two approaches to life. Which approach do you prefer? Explain why.

You should write at least 250 words.

GENERAL TRAINING TASK 2: #74

You should spend about 40 minutes on this task.

Do you agree or disagree with the following statement?
Businesses should do anything they can to make a profit.
Use specific reasons and examples to support your position.

You should write at least 250 words.

GENERAL TRAINING TASK 2: #75

You should spend about 40 minutes on this task.

All education, primary, secondary and further education, should be free to all people and paid for by the government.

Do you agree or disagree with this statement?

You should write at least 250 words.

GENERAL TRAINING TASK 2: #76

You should spend about 40 minutes on this task.

The 21st century has begun. What changes do you think this new century will bring?
Use examples and details in your answer.

You should write at least 250 words.

GENERAL TRAINING TASK 2: #77

You should spend about 40 minutes on this task.

Some people prefer to plan activities for their free time very carefully. Others choose not to make any plans at all for their free time. Compare the benefits of planning free-time activities with the benefits of not making plans.
Which do you prefer - planning or not planning for your leisure time?
Use specific reasons and examples to explain your choice.

You should write at least 250 words.

GENERAL TRAINING TASK 2: #78

You should spend about 40 minutes on this task.

Do you agree or disagree with the following statement?
Advertising can tell you a lot about a country.

Use specific reasons and examples to support your answer.

You should write at least 250 words.

GENERAL TRAINING TASK 2: #79

You should spend about 40 minutes on this task.

Some people say that advertising encourages us to buy things we really do not need. Others say that advertisements tell us about new products that may improve our lives. Which viewpoint do you agree with?

Use specific reasons and examples to support your answer.

You should write at least 250 words.

GENERAL TRAINING TASK 2: #80

You should spend about 40 minutes on this task.

Some people like to do only what they already do well.
Other people prefer to try new things and take risks. Which do you prefer?
Use specific reasons and examples to support your choice.

You should write at least 250 words.

IELTS Sample Charts (IELTS Writing Task 1)

The Writing Task 1 of the IELTS Academic test requires you to write a summary of at least 150 words in response to a particular graph (bar, line or pie graph), table, chart, or process (how something works, how something is done). This task tests your ability to select and report the main features, to describe and compare data, identify significance and trends in factual information, or describe a process.

You are assessed on :

- Task Achievement (how well you answer the question)
- Coherence and Cohesion
- Lexical Resource (use of appropriate vocabulary)
- Grammatical Range and Accuracy (the accuracy and range of the grammar you use)

Task 2 or Task 1 first ?

Students frequently ask whether they should do Task 1 first or Task 2. This obviously depends on the individual. It is probably wise, however, to do Task 1 first. From the psychological point of view, it gives you a sense of accomplishment when you have finished it.

Note that the value of the marks given to each Task is reflected in the time. There are twice as many marks for Task 2 as for Task 1. The marks are combined to produce one Band Score from 1 to 9 for the whole test. Note also that if you write less than 150 words for Task 1 and less than 250 for Task 2, you will lose marks.

IELTS Writing Task 1 Review

What information is Writing Task 1 based on?
Data presented as a table, graph (bar or pie chart) or a diagram.

How do you have to express the information?
Concisely and accurately.

Does it matter whether you use an informal style?
You should not use an informal style; you should write in a formal and academic style.

Are grammar, spelling and punctuation tested?
Yes, you should make sure you use a range of grammatical structures and try to be accurate.

How long should you spend on this task?
About 20 minutes.

How many words must you write?
At least 150.

Which parts of the data must you write about?
The most important or noticeable features, trends or points.

Should you make comparisons?
Yes, when appropriate.

What should you draw attention to and interpret?
Features of the data.

IELTS Writing Tip

Write a brief introduction in your own words using information from the question and the headings or text. For example, include an overview statement about what the data shows. After that, you should focus on key trends, main features and details. Every main feature should be supported by figures from the data. The report should finish with a short summary.

Do not speculate or offer an opinion that is outside the given data. Also, you do not need to describe every single change shown in the data, but describe the overall trends. General observations must be supported with specific examples from the data.

Use a variety of language to describe trends - for example, verbs with adverbs and nouns with adjectives. The examiner will want to see whether you can deal with the task with flexibility and precision. Showing your ability to use a wide range of vocabulary accurately and appropriately will help you get a higher score for your writing.

Do not copy the wording in the exam question. If you do, these words will be deducted from the total number of words and will not be assessed.

Easy ways to improve and expand your vocabulary

Seven Tips for Learning New Words

Communicate (speak and write) more clearly and concisely using these seven tips for learning new words... easy ways to improve and expand your vocabulary.
by Randall S. Hansen, Ph.D.
Looking for tips for improving your vocabulary? Whether you are trying to strengthen and broaden your vocabulary for school or personal growth, the key is a commitment to regularly learning new words.
Why expand your knowledge and use of words? You'll be able to communicate (speak and write) more clearly and concisely, people will understand you more easily, and you will increase the perception (and reality) that you are an intelligent person. Besides, learning new words is a fun activity -- and one you can even do with the people around you. Challenge a friend, family member, or roommate to learn new words with you.
This article reviews seven easy ways to improve your vocabulary and learn new words.

1. Read, read, and read. The more you read -- especially novels and literary works, but also magazines and newspapers -- the more words you'll be exposed to. As you read and uncover new words, use a combination of attempting to derive meaning from the context of the sentence as well as from looking up the definition in a dictionary.

2. Keep a dictionary and thesaurus handy. Use whatever versions you prefer -- in print, software, or online. When you uncover a new word, look it up in the dictionary to get both its pronunciation and its meaning(s). Next, go to the thesaurus and find similar words and phrases -- and their opposites (synonyms and antonyms, respectively) -- and learn the nuances among the words.

3. Use a journal. It's a good idea to keep a running list of the new words you discover so that you can refer back to the list and slowly build them into your everyday vocabulary. Plus, keeping a journal of all your new words can provide positive reinforcement for learning even more words -- especially when you can see how many new words you've already learned.

4. Learn a word a day. Using a word-a-day calendar or Website -- or developing your own list of words to learn -- is a great technique many people use to learn new words. This approach may be too rigid for some, so even if you do use this method, don't feel you must learn a new word every day. (Find some word-a-day Websites at the end of this article.)

5. Go back to your roots. One of the most powerful tools for learning new words -- and for deciphering the meaning of other new words -- is studying Latin and Greek roots. Latin and Greek elements (prefixes, roots, and suffixes) are a significant part of the English language and a great tool for learning new words. (Follow these links for the sections of this site that provide English Vocabulary Derived from Latin and English Vocabulary Derived from Greek.)

6. Play some games. Word games that challenge you and help you discover new meanings and new words are a great and fun tool in your quest for expanding your vocabulary. Examples include crossword puzzles, anagrams, word jumble, Scrabble, and Boggle. (Find some word-game Websites at the end of this article.)

7. Engage in conversations. Simply talking with other people can help you learn discover new words. As with reading, once you hear a new word, remember to jot it down so that you can study it later -- and then slowly add the new word to your vocabulary.

Final Thoughts On Improving and Expanding Your Vocabulary

You hold the key to a better vocabulary. By using the tips outlined , you should be well on your way to discovering and learning new words to expand your vocabulary and strengthen your use of the English language.

Finally, remember that you must practice putting your new words into your writing and speaking or risk not retaining them in your brain. Use repetition exercises when you first learn a word -- and consider other learning techniques, such as index cards, recording yourself reciting your words, association games, and mnemonics.

IELTS Band Scores

9 Expert user:
has fully operational command of the language: appropriate, accurate and fluent with complete understanding.

8 Very good user:
has fully operational command of the language with only occasional unsystematic inaccuracies and inappropriacies. Misunderstandings may occur in unfamiliar situations. Handles complex detailed argumentation well.

7 Good user:
has operational command of the language, though with occasional inaccuracies, inappropriacies and misunderstandings in some situations. Generally handles complex language well and understands detailed reasoning.

6 Competent user:
has generally effective command of the language despite some inaccuracies, inappropriacies and misunderstandings. Can use and understand fairly complex language, particularly in familiar situations.

5 Modest user:
has partial command of the language, coping with overall meaning in most situations, though is likely to make many mistakes. Should be able to handle basic communication in own field.

4 Limited user:
basic competence is limited to familiar situations. Has frequent problems in understanding and expression. Is not able to use complex language.

3 Extremely limited:
conveys and understands only general meaning in very familiar situations. Frequent breakdowns in communication occur.

2 Intermittent user:
no real communication is possible except for the most basic information using isolated words or short formulae in familiar situations and to meet immediate needs. Has great difficulty understanding spoken and written English.

1 Non-user:
essentially has no ability to use the language beyond possibly a few isolated words.

0 Did not attempt:
No assessable information provided.

Made in the USA
Middletown, DE
27 November 2020